First Stars

Jay Klokker

First Stars

Jay Klokker

Irene Weinberger Books
An Imprint of Hamilton Stone Editions
Maplewood, New Jersey

Library of Congress Cataloging-in-Publication Data

Names: Klokker, Jay, 1953- author.
Title: First stars / Jay Klokker.
Other titles: First stars (Compilation)
Description: Maplewood, New Jersey : Irene Weinberger Books, an
        Imprint of Hamilton Stone Editions [2023] | Summary: "First
        Stars is a collection of lyric poems about fathers and nature
        and the natural course of life,
including one's own confrontations with endings"-- Provide by
    publisher.

Identifiers: LCCN 2023014435 | ISBN 9781736500132 (trade
        paperback)
Subjects: LCGFT: Poetry.
Classification: LCC PS3611.L64 F57 2023 | DDC 811/.6--dc23/eng/
        20230510
LC record available at https://lccn.loc.gov/2023014435

Irene Weinberger Books
An Imprint of Hamilton Stone Editions
Maplewood, New Jersey
ireneweinbergerbooks.com
hamiltonstone.org

Cover art by Iliana Melissis
Book Design by WSM

Dedication

To all of my teachers, including
the ones who thought they were my students—
and most of all, and forever, to Ingrid

Table of Contents

Seeing Stars

All of your life
you've been pressing

your luck and the heels
of your hands to your eyes.

The harder you press
the brighter the phosphenes

appear to be burning—
they are the stars

the comic strip villain sees
linking hands

high overhead in a circle
of dizzying steps.

You have watched him
set a box-trap

at the base of a cliff.
You have rooted for him

knowing full well
he will never look up

in time to dodge the falling
sofa or safe or piano.

You have said to yourself
when will he learn?

Now open your eyes.
Think of what new

constellations have formed
overnight. What sky.

What space you have opened
your eyes upon.

Section One:
Arcturus

Amphibians

After a long desert hike
      my father's feet, as pale
as a pair of cave salamanders

slide out of his socks
      into the cool green waters of
the irrigation ditch—

where my feet, mottled pink,
      peeling with sunburn, are
wriggling in the mud:

I could stay here forever, my father
      doesn't say—
Yes, let's, I don't reply, our silences

as always fitting together
      while the silt, that ghostly
enlivening ooze, massages

the tender
      knots of flesh
between our toes.

My Father's Leg: The Story

In the story I grew up with,
     my father and two other boys
with shotguns hunting squirrels

in the gold Wisconsin woods
     were hopping crossties of
a train track and tightrope-walking

its gleaming steel rail
     when one boy missed his step,
shot my father

in the leg and ran away,
     while the other boy
hightailed it to town—

leaving my father alone
     in those woods
with nothing but the stem

of his tobacco pipe to twist
     his bright blue bandana
into the tourniquet

that kept him alive.

The Heart Needs No Roof
—for Manuel O., who stargazed

Because the house where
your dreams became real
had stone walls and no roof
to block its view of the volcano
even now there come nights
when the ceiling of your bedroom
dissolves and you're seven years old
keeping watch until dawn
while the night-singing birds
and blood-sucking assassin bugs
draw shadows of red across
the face of the moon.

Dangerous Facts

When pressed to explain what I feel, I remember the time I ran home from school crying because I thought everyone there could read minds. I'd been trying to show them the difference between the sailbacked reptile edaphosaurus and the similar, but fiercer, dimetredon, when I realized they were listening, not to me, but to a part of my voice that I couldn't hear. I tried to distract them with dangerous facts: how many apple seeds it takes to kill a man and how to make a sleeping potion from urine. Imagine yourself, I said, lying in bed on the surface of a white dwarf star. Try lifting your finger. It weighs one thousand two hundred pounds. Now open your eyelids—if you can find them. Your brain, I said, is nothing but soup with chunks of bone in it. That's when the teacher sent me home with a note saying, "Your child has a problem with peer interaction." I wanted to ask my mother if this was like a chemical interaction, but I was afraid she would lie. That night I couldn't get to sleep. I had to know the facts about everything.

Billy the Kid Bites the Dust

When Johnny threw the rock, I didn't duck.
Why should I? The rock looked like a dirt clod
and Billy the Kid doesn't duck dirt clods;
he stands tall, he stands his ground, he tells Doc
Holliday, You ain't tough! But then the rock
and Johnny yelling, Oh shit! hit my head.

Was I knocked out? Did I lie in the dirt
and dream I was dead, like those careless kids
our teacher scared us with: that show-off
who dove into a drained swimming pool,
that girl throttled by a tetherball serve?
Did Johnny plead with God to let me live?

Maybe. All I know is next time we played
Wild West Showdown, Johnny was the Kid.

The Windbeast, 1962

That night when Seattle went dark
and the Space Needle wobbled
and a Coast Guard anemometer measured
a hundred seventy nine miles per hour
before it broke—

That night when airplanes lost their wings
and cattle got crushed under barn roofs
and a Volkswagen bug tumbled end over end
in a suburb where a paperboy flew and a pair
of soggy lions escaped—

That night while the house shuddered
and I stood in my PJs in the living room
in the candle-lit dark
I wasn't scared—

                I was amazed to see
the plate-glass window bellying inward
all that storm holding its breath
       its flank quivering
to be stroked.

Missing Cuckoo Grandma

Back when clocks had faces
my brother's kids called mom
cuckoo grandma because her house
was where they hoisted clock weights
and twiddled stubby clock hands
to keep the cuckoo on time.

*

In the dining room
where the cuckoo clock hung
mom stuck out her tongue to show
the diamond-shaped scar
her brother gave her
when she dared him to shut
the bathroom door in her face

and he did.

*

In my dream, the moon
cuckooed in the dining room
and the cuckoo clock
dawdled in the sky,
sticking out a wooden
tongue shaped like a spoon.

*

Mom, cuckoo grandma,
after all these years,
let's go outside and make faces—
let's stick our time-tattered
tongues out at the moon.

The Accordionist

When my mother had the blues
she'd have me play
The Battle Hymn of the Republic
and while the faithful chords
marched on from major to diminished
and my fingers squeezed the bellows
where the grapes of wrath are stored
her upper lip would quiver
and she'd let herself be sad.

How I hated it. Those afternoons
I played that patriotic march
I tried to lose it in a jungle of grace notes
and chords that swelled until
you couldn't tell what they started as.
The tune was something like a cross
between John Philip Sousa and a car crash
and still she'd say, *That's nice*
and *I feel much better now.*
Yes, I felt bad
     but I enjoyed
pretending that   I didn't want
   to please her—
      I liked the game of giving
her her song and marching it
   about-face into jazz.

How much I didn't know.
I didn't see my mother'd gone inside herself
and was sitting in front of a bandstand
waiting for her dad the mayor to give a speech.
I didn't hear her favorite teacher hiss:
That damn Georgenson's a Red.

We never talked politics, but when I asked
if Manitowoc had ever had a Socialist for mayor,
she dug out a scrapbook of clippings
and laughed: *I should have known
I couldn't keep a secret from my nosey son.*

How she must have loved the light that skimmed
the trumpets when they were lifted
toward the sky—
                                 and when their song of glory
blasted forth
                          the battle it called her to
was not the one that raged with napalm in my dreams.

She didn't see the horror closing in
when choppers cleared the line of Douglas firs
between us and the snow-capped Olympics.
She didn't see the new war taking shape.

In the year I held my breath while dates of birth
were being drawn, my mother called herself
a spunky little squib and bragged of
ripping a sign from a protestor's hands.
I didn't ask what the sign had said
or if she'd seen my face
among the faces at the march.
There wasn't, I thought, any point
in bringing up our differences.

Now something has changed
to make me see love must go
where understanding stops.
Yes, I still hate brass bands
and haven't played the accordion
in decades, but when I think
of my mother, my fingers touch
the keys and I say

             Yes, I'll play that song
       I'll play it note for note
I'll play until the fateful lightning's loosed
          and truth comes marching in
                all song
          all Glory Glory Hallelujah—
I'll play until we both hear
          what we love
                and who we are

Shaving My Father

The very thought makes me nervous—
I fill the blue pan
with hot water, set it
on the nightstand
and watch him   his hand pressing
                              the pillow, his breathing

so hard he seems to be covered in breath

*

He used to say
Nothing comes easy
now I see
he hasn't shaved all week;
he needs me to help him with his face.

So I begin.
I stir the towel
in the water, then wring.
                              I wrap
                              his cheeks, softening
                              also the chin.
I do not cover
the opening lips

                              while behind them the tongue
                              is unable to press
the hollows out
and lift up the half-hidden stubble.

*

                              With his head tipped
                              back on the pillow
what does he feel
          as I lather the face
          and what
                              as I snap
                              the disposable razor
                              free of its package?

*

Remember I need to say
to myself this hair
is a harvest   but only as harvest means work
                                                        and the time for it
which is now:

                                I am setting the razor down
on the cheek,
the angle just right
                                        I am pulling into the suds
                                                always into the grain
I am changing directions
for the cheek-bone,
the jawbone

                                I am rinsing the blade again
                                and again the suds are
floating
        speckled with gray
and a few spots of red—

                                Not bad   I am thinking
not bad, but yet
        there's the tough, the fresh
vulnerability of the throat.

                                This neck, would he know it
as the one he craned
        in the mirror maneuvering
the skin under the blade?

                                *

                                When he turns
                        to the press
                                of my hand I want to say

27

everything is
as it always has been
and I want him to feel how ordinary
all this is: the water cooling
in the basin, clotted   with hair and dappled
                                    just slightly
                         with blood.

                              *

Perhaps even as I pour the water
into the sink he will be clearing his throat
making way for a word

Perhaps I will be watching the suds
catch at the drain lip
                         when I hear it, that word
                              I can't quite imagine

And I turn toward the bed
        where his voice is gently shaking
              shaking me back into the world

                         back here

                    where his voice has been stopped
               and he needs me more
                         to wipe the soap from his face
          than I need to hear
               the sound my name made
                    when he was calling me

Section Two:
Ursa Majoris

In Bear Country

It was late summer in Yosemite
and I was a young man with a red canvas pack
climbing the switchbacks to Tuolumne Meadows.
I had just quit my job and thought being alone
with the mountains would help me discover
what to do with my life.

For three days I was happy
unrolling my sleeping bag on pine needles
with nothing to do but keep the river company,
teach myself the recorder, and read aloud
from the one book I had, a coverless paperback
a truckdriver had thrust in my hands saying:
Be good to the goodness inside you,
open your heart to the Lord.

On the fourth morning I found paw prints
superimposed on my footsteps as if
left by a creature who wears half a boot
and has claws. I remembered what
the park ranger said about *nuisance bears,*
so used to being fed they'll crawl into
your tent to eat a candy bar or to lick
peppermint toothpaste from your lips.
That night, after my freeze-dried tetrazzini,
I rehung my foodsack from a higher limb.

I can't say what woke me. All I remember
are shadows coalescing into the shape
of a bear, its muzzle so close to my face
I could have stroked behind its ears.
Don't panic, I said to myself. *It's only*
a black bear, it's bound to be more scared
than you are. Unzip your sleeping bag.
Wave your arms to make yourself look big.

But the zipper got stuck and I pictured what
the bear must have seen: a giant blue worm.
Which part would it choose to eat first?
The head? The flapping appendages?
Or would it go straight for the heart?

It's a good thing my body remembered
what a small, cornered animal does to survive.
Like an orgasm storming the body, sound
leapt from my throat taking its own sweet time
taking me out of the self that loves words
and is careful and has to make sense of things
so that it can separate *dangerous* from *good*.
But here there was nothing to separate, nothing but
the wail in my ears and the one in my throat.

The next thing I knew there was silence
and pink light was touching the cliffs.
Only a dream, I told myself,
it was only a dream... A message in code
from one part of myself to another.
Not till I went to make breakfast
did I see that my dream could climb trees
and had claws to rip a foodsack to shreds.

With nothing to eat but a sprinkling of rice
peppered with half-inch black hairs
what could I do but pack up and leave?
By late afternoon I was smiling at traffic
and sticking out my thumb.
I wasn't sure where I was going
but I trusted the future to take me there.

Remembering the Skykomish
—for Richard Hugo

The Sky is the same gray river it was
when it hummed in your ear each November,
and the winter-run steelhead still leap
as their bodies beat the air into silver
at the end of drunk fishermen's lines.
Not like coho that spawn once then die,

these seagoing trout come back year after year
to the riffles and pools of the streambed
where you and your friends waded toward them
threading red skeins of fish egg on hooks.
Fishing, wrote Orwell, is the opposite of war,
but Orwell never waded hip-deep in the Sky

or felt at home with the stone-colored clouds,
the cold slap of wind, the green blur of cedar
through a mist where the men stand in rows
in the water like the pilings of a dismantled pier
or a bridge that will never be complete.
Bleak landscapes were always your favorites

and steelheading gave you the perfect excuse
to blend into the rain on a sand bar
or take shelter in a deer poacher's shack—
its one window papered with news clippings
recounting a murder the police left unsolved
when no one could identify the victim. That's

life, you showed us, an unfinished business
where the best we can do is to pay close
attention to whatever the world has to show.
If it gives us a river, we stand by the river
reading the current and trying to think
like the steelhead nosing its way past our bait.

Whale Watch
—for Wendy Battin

On the way out we watch cormorants
ride low in the water and swivel
their heads, living periscopes
sizing us up. Gulls keen in our wake
while petrels and shearwaters usher us
past fogbanks and kelp-shrouded reefs
into the humpback feeding ground.

With the thrum of its engine cut off,
our boat Ariel drifts, rocking gently,
lulling us with the same
ocean swells that once rocked
wooden whaleboats while
harpooneers cocked their arms.

Look! squawks the *Ariel's* bullhorn:
off starboard lies
                        the footprint of a whale—
and so we, who a moment ago were fumbling
with binoculars or popping dramamine
or rounding up the kids for a group selfie,
stare at an undulating patch

of stillness the shape of a life raft
and strain to feel the stirrings of a song
pitched to underwater ears—
a song of how, while we were looking
elsewhere, a forty-ton humpback
leapt into the air—
                        and for a

moment flew.

One Morning Running

along North Bend Road
I picked up a raven's wingfeather

from the grass, and ran on,
and when the welder's black dog

snarled and chased me faster
than I could run, I watched the feather

tremble in my hand while the dog
sniffed it sideways and lengthwise

before wagging the luxurious
raven plume of a tail.

My Father's Leg: The Pen Knife

My father wears his Humphrey Bogart
poker face and sits on the couch
surrounded by Boy Scouts curious
to see why one of his legs isn't straight.
He doesn't explain. He lifts the cuff
of his khaki work pants and asks,
"How many of you boys have shot
a shotgun?"

       None answer,
but all watch as he furls the cuff
over his knee, revealing a hole
the diameter of a pencil lead.
"That's where the pellets went in,"
he says, "And here is
where—

                most of them came out."
A couple scouts pretend to look away,
but most stare at the edge of the crater
carved through the flesh and bone
of my father's thigh, where his fingertip rolls
what looks like a water-rounded pebble
lodged under the oysterish skin
of his inner leg.

All this happened before I was born,
when my brother was one of those scouts.
Or maybe not. All I'm almost sure of
is that Dad plucked the pellet free
with the same agate-handled penknife
he used years later to slice apples in half,
gut trout, and once at the seashore
to carve shards of broken bottle from my palm
while I made myself hold still
and heard the ocean roar in my head.

The Colonization of Planet B

We hermit crabs feel right at home
In zero G, shedding snail-suits
And floating bare-assed in a dream
Of eelgrass worlds and Martian whales.
Our navigator crab exhales
Sideways: "New Terra, here we come!"
Then cabin fever, busted claws,
Busted airlocks, Earth just a crumb

Of glimmer in a sea of gloom
While Captain Cork's sabre-claw flails
And red-zones the reactor room
Where our space-phobic AI fails
Again to fix the solar sails—
What next? Who's left to beam us home?

Because the Human Heart is 70% Water

grandmother water   ocean of us all sings us alive
sings us lullabies that   blossom into dreams into

once upon a time   on a planet with two suns and no moon
a robot gave birth to   a dust storm named thirst
and wherever thirst went   thirst remembered being called

by another name   a damp salty tangle of syllables
impossible to pronounce   and yet echoing riptides and jellyfish
skies flooded with auroras   music beckoning

music reckoning   with yet another once upon a time
after time shed its skin   and breath crystalized into words
into robots and dust storms   into lullabies of how

even on the knife-edge of thirst   the heart is the water
knot grandmother ocean   cinches tight in us all

The Chair

Evening. December. A man
has just left this room, this red
and green cubicle, for the other room,
the one with the sunflowers on the yellow wall.

Soon he will be back. Soon
he will take up what he left
on the cushion: two half-read novels
and a candle in a small black bowl.

The rim of the bowl is gold enamel,
the candle the one white object in the room.
Soon the two friends will start to talk
and the words will be electric between them.

To listen to their voices intertwine
is to watch the apostrophe of flame
freeze in the shape of a keyhole.
The air opens inward, and the past

is a cottage where two friends have argued
and one of them reaches for a knife.
But no one is hurt. Not yet.
That will come after

the chair has been set
by the table and the candle snuffed out
and one of the books has dropped free
from its hand, opening itself to the floor.

—after a painting by Van Gogh

Trakl Under Fire (1914)

While the wind rose
        and windfalls fell
the medical lieutenant walked
        the orchard path
where bruised apples pitched
        small tents of shade—
the quiet of no morning gunfire
        was a newsy letter from home
the wind recited
        as he filled his knapsack up.

He gave the apples away
        to cheer the wounded, then
worse-wounded came, ninety
        bullet-savaged bodies impossible
        to save or relieve—ninety broken
nightmare mouths cursing God.

That night shivering on
        the precipice of sleep,
he clutched an apple he pet-named
        Divinity's Betrayal—
and whenever fresh gunshots
        or whimpers of pain
shook his bones, he bit
        deep into apple flesh,
inhaling sweet cider breath
        the way a patient inhales
chloroform before the cutting starts

My Father's Leg: In Lieu of an Elegy

Death has many doors: some bullet-scarred,
some latched with a shoestring, some welded shut,
some unhinged, some waiting to be nudged
open by a push broom.

*

Are you okay?
                         So said the janitor when he
surprised my father in the men's room standing on one leg,
clutching the bent knee of the other leg
to his chest;
                         Yes, my father said, embarrassed to be caught
perched like a flamingo, *I'm okay,*
and then, as he lowered his foot and straightened up,
the pain of an almost burst appendix
came unpent.

*

I nearly died, my father said, and after years
of practicing how to be okay with being not okay
that's what he did.

Lucifer's Final Soliloquy

Lullaby master, lullaby and farewell,
your wish is no longer my command, your bacchanal
no longer my affair. Your guardian angel
is resigning his post, and the Gordian knot
of your wanting everything then wanting something else
is a bird's nest for you to unsnarl with your teeth.
I suppose you thought omnipotence would be easy?
Clever monkey, ingratiating Lord of all creatures,
you can have your dominion, just go back to sleep
and let dreams unroll blueprints for Genesis.
Tomorrow you can call in your day laborers
and there shall be, if you want, exaltations of seraphim
to navigate the cut crystal stars in their spheres.
Or perhaps you'll turn the key of the Enlightenment
contraption with its mainspring and offbalanced
flywheels giving spin to a labyrinth of gears.
Whatever you do won't require my assistance.
There'll be left a few questions of genealogy,
some subcommittees of creationists to boss around,
and a few prophets to send on wild dove chases,
but, let's face it, eternity is mostly loose ends.
I don't know how you plan to cope with the tedium,
but if I were in your place, I'd hire a sharp team
of ghost writers, or write myself into a long-running
situation comedy with pratfalls and billions of extras.
As for that brimstone everlasting and hellfire project—
lullaby master, lullaby and good luck,
my keys are on the table. Don't stay in touch.

Section Three:
Venus

Political Economy

If a stone in the hand gathers no moss

     and the going rate for ungathered moss

is two birds per bush with each bird doing

     piecework seven days a week no overtime

no sick leave stitching nine saved stitches per day

     assuming you to be a conscientious haystack

how many stones does your needle cost?

The Coalminer Caught Unawares

Thinking it safe to dream as he worked
because the wedge tapped into the crack
of the overhead seam would, if it fell, wake him,
he looked into the dark and saw

what he wished for: the orchard, with Katerina
alive once again, shuffling windfalls
into her apron, while he plucked from the branch
above her and thought how her breasts

would weigh in his hands. Watching her comb
through the grass, he wanted to labor
beside her forever, whispering of a land
where apples turn to stone, and stone burns.

Then her hand brushed his cheek.
Katerina? he said. But she was gone,
and the orchard as well, all its
apple boughs breaking into beams.

"I Never Had Seen a Tomato"
—from a story my father's father told

First day in from Copenhagen,
he circled the market for hours, glad
the sidewalk planks didn't sway or slap.
Their firmness made him remember
how his plowstride fit the earth.

With each step in front of the last
creating the gradual curve of a furrow,
he rounded the city corners, thinking,
hoping for something—
                         apples
                it must have been
          because there they were, heaped red
     in the basket in the market, and like everything else
so much brighter here.
                   For a farmer
in need of a harvest, however small,
it was worth a whole nickel to rub his palm
against appleskin all afternoon and feel
how smoothness grows smoother
in a smooth climate, with a soft give,
yet unspoiled.

Despite what came next—
the bite of disappointment,
the pulp spat out—
anticipation is what
sustained him.

Thaw

The snowman half-melted in the sun
looks more human than before—

with the head gone, the torso looks
so like a head bowed in prayer

I feel the winter inside of me
bubbling with laughter and blessed.

The Hug

A month after my stepson fled to Paris
and hanged himself in a public park,
I was waiting for the F train to take me
to a party with friends in Brooklyn
where all talk of mental illness
and suicide had been banned.
Busy rehearsing small talk
and trying not to think of
Aaron's death, I didn't see who was
making the rounds of the platform
till a hand bumped my shoulder
and a big moon-faced man gazed
down at me. Ducking his head,
the man mumbled a request as
inaudible as the asides
Aaron muttered to prove he wasn't
duped by benevolence. Homeless,
he called himself when he lived with us,
homeless, like the man in the ripped parka
booming, "Bless you, my child!" as I filled
his palm with all the change I had, then waited
for him to walk away. The man frowned.
"Aren't you forgetting something?"
How was I to answer? It was like
hearing Aaron ask, "What brand of poison are
you serving today?" and remembering how
he once broke down a door.
The man shook his head. Slowly.
Sadly. Disapprovingly. "Son," he said,
"did you ever know me to beat
you for no reason?" All I could think
to say was "No."
"So where is my hug?"
I didn't move, but already strong arms
pulled me close and my cheek thumped
the pillow of a down-padded chest.
"I'm God," the man confided. "And you—
you and Malcolm X are my sons."
How crazy, I thought, how crazy that
my muscles in that instant unclenched

and a sob caught in my throat as if
it was Aaron's hurt I held close
and Aaron hugging back
before both of us let go.

Time Machine
—for Iliana

After you told me your teacher is making you write poems
you showed me the dirt-flecked grey Olympia portable
you got for free at the second-hand store and while we
rethreaded the red-and-black typewriter ribbon and tested
the keys (all working except the comma) the words
carriage return popped into my head and I was back
at the left-hand margin of early adulthood Colorado
where I had been last seen sitting on the floor
hunched over my almost-brand-new
grey Olympia portable typewriter clacking away
at what I still hope will turn out to be a poem.

Breakfast Mind
—for David Walker

The dad dancing in
the kitchen in a purple
tie-dyed tee-shirt
that says Zen Dad!
isn't a real zen dad—

       and is

Waiting for the Diagnosis

Get it right!
>   *Get it right!*
Get it right right right!—

So sings the chickadee
as it flits from the dogwood
to the rhododendron
and so frets the overloaded
brain:

>   *Get it right!*
Get it right!
>   *Get it right right right!*

The brain wants a world
where thinking doesn't hurt
and understanding sings
truth into the heart
and what the brain gets is—

Got it wrong?
>   sings the chickadee
and the brain cocks an ear

>   then as brains do
sings along.

Uncle

About you i know next to nothing

only that you had my father's name before
it was anglicized and handed down to him

only that you died as a baby or maybe as
the big-headed toddler whose picture
spilled out of a shoebox of old photographs

only that something twisted in your bowels
and you wailed for three days and three nights
and grandma would have followed you into the grave
if a neighbor lady hadn't made sure that she ate

only that the neighbor lady's last name
probably was mongo because mongo was
the middle name my father tried to keep secret

only that you were born and died
in texas farm country near brownsville
unless it was galveston or san antonio

only that i have no idea who told me
about you and how much of what i know
i made up

only that you were loved.

Shaving the Ghost

An old man shaving
      nicks his chin and hears
his dead father sigh, sees
      the trembling ghost of
his father's hand reach
      behind the mirror for
the stinging styptic pencil
      that got dumped in the trash
fifty years ago—

The man wishes he had that
      fat pencil now and could
chalk his bloody chin white
      instead of rubbing it numb
with an ice cube and sporting
      a toilet paper goatee.

Though he can't stop hearing his father
      say *What's wrong with you?*
the eyes in the mirror—
      the serious deep-set brown eyes
he inherited—crinkle at the corners
      when he waggles his chin.

Hi Dad, he says
      and watches
his father's eyes laugh.

My Father's Leg: Didn't He

He didn't make much of it. Gritted
his teeth. Put his hands on his knees
and caught his breath a little longer
when he set down his end of the canoe
at the lake edge. Didn't talk about
crawling through the belly of a battleship
breathing asbestos for the war effort.
Didn't say where he hurt most.
Didn't stop smoking. Didn't curse.
And then came the dinner when he
pushed away his blackberry cobbler
with ice cream and said, "I have no regrets."
He didn't say anything more.

Love

After he died, the first thing she got rid of
was the handgun a friend had talked him into buying
so she could stay safe on her own.
She was sure the wrong person would get shot.

His bourbon went next. After years of
mixing highballs to help him unclinch
when his cough got the best of him
she wasn't about to start drinking alone.

Then came the work of scrubbing tobacco
tar stains from the walls and painting
the walls eggshell white until the house
was aired out, and at last she felt free

from death's stench. Still, she couldn't bear
to get rid of a pair of his pajamas,
steeped in cigarette smoke and sweat,
tucked under her pillow, ready for nights

when she woke up afraid, nights when she
burrowed her nose into the smell of him, picturing how
he would chuckle at her foolishness,
his love washing over her until she fell asleep.

First Stars
—for Ingrid

No moon, no clouds between us and the dark,
we trace the Milky Way's glittering sweep
and follow the Big Dipper's handle to
where Arcturus is hiding in the trees.

Arcturus, I say, was the first star I learned.
and ask what was yours. Venus, you say,
your laughter the laugh of a little girl
with long braids walking home from a friend's.

How she dawdles while the sunset darkens
from apricot to plum, how she stands on
tiptoe to look past a hedge—all this is
in-breath, then she intones: Star light, star bright...
shaping from her heart's whispered wish a life
she can't imagine, this night that we love.

Afterthoughts

I want to say how grateful I am for my poetry writers peer group, Hillary Gardner, Ingrid Blaufarb Hughes, Gary Keenan, Jamie O'Halloran and Weslea Sidon. We had years of fulfilling support and critiquing that helped strengthen and polish my poems. Not only did the group encourage my work, it helped me see when a poem was finished and avoid overthinking it. They embodied the very best qualities of literary critiquing and friendship.

–Jay Klokker

*

This book of tightly focused, thematically linked poems on the themes of memory, mortality, and imagination is the result of a lifetime devoted to poetry and poets. The calm clarity of the voice is Jay Klokker's alone as he considers what he recalls versus what he comes to recognize in the moments of the poem's arrival and completion. The shared discoveries animate a profound connection to the reader as the poems lend their prismatic light to meanings that inhabit our world, one image, one word at a time. As a fortunate colleague and friend of Jay's for forty years, I read these poems with awe and wonder for the process that yielded them and how deeply that process has informed my own life as a writer and man. Take time with such poems as they mark their own time. It will be time well spent.

—Gary Keenan

Gary Keenan is the author of Rotary Devotion, which won the 2017 Poets Out Loud Award and is available from Fordham University Press.

*

I have met very few people I would call a real mensch. Jay is one. To be a real mensch is to exemplify the best humanity has to offer—kindness, inclusiveness, dignity, sincerity. Each year for the last decade or so, Jay has given me a work day—help cleaning out the mess my husband and I create in our continual acquisitiveness. The quality of menschness shines on those days. I am lifted out of my own negative self-judgements by Jay's lack of them.

Jay's qualities of real menschness gave shape and depth to our poetry group. His critiques are the result of total attention to the poems presented. Every word in every poem is treated with respect. His vast knowledge of the craft is always presented in service to the poem. His open-hearted acceptance, and sometimes rejection, of our critiques are little masterclasses in how to improve craft.

My poems, my barn, and my life are all a little better because of Jay's input. All I can say about that is thank you.

—Weslea Sidon

Weslea Sidon is the author of *The Fool Sings* from Rain Chain Press.

*

When I think of Jay, I think of running into him at "Jay Street" in downtown Brooklyn, near the F train stop at Metro Tech. For over fifteen years, he and I were adult literacy educators together at the City University of New York. If I visited him in his classroom at City Tech, I'd have to negotiate the bustling plazas and wide Tillary Street with its crazy countdown crosswalk signal reminding pedestrians they might never make it across...

These were the same streets that Walt Whitman used to tromp in the "age of go-ahead." Like Whitman, Jay, a keen observer, delights in human enjoyment and lived experience; he believes art can be a force for good. How lucky to match Jay's stride as he headed for Greene Acres Community Garden in Bed-Stuy with a group of students who have read free books on growing food for World Book Night. For Jay, there was never a "too far out of the way."

A dedicated teacher, Jay is also inquisitive and fearless as a writer. When he volunteered to join me for 30 Poems in November, a fundraising effort for the Center for New Americans and a marathon of creativity for a good cause, we decided to see if we could write thirty poems all in one day. Jay sent me "seeds," small ideas with which to form haiku. Write, he requested: Who are your people, how did you travel, what is the most important souvenir?

In the subway, we rumble as though underwater, schools of travelers, rushing throngs of strangers. Out of the commotion of getting home, someone recognizes me, someone who always seems calm and kind. Someone with a voice that moves at a measured pace. Someone who is curious, exacting, and interested in what is going on today. Jay.

—Hillary Gardner

Hillary Gardner is a poet and translator.

*

In one of the poems here, 'Remembering the Skykomish', Jay addresses the late poet Richard Hugo:

> ...That's
> life, you showed us, an unfinished business
> where the best we can do is to pay
> close attention to whatever the world has to show.

In these lines, Jay addresses all of us. His close attention to the natural world, the political world, each of us, is his strength as a poet and as a human being.

Jay and I met in Nelson Bentley's poetry workshop at the University of Washington in 1977. Jay's intellect and imagination were obvious. As our friendship grew, a friendship I treasure, I felt the kindness and compassion in Jay's core, qualities evident in these poems. Jay and I stayed in touch, mostly through letters which were folded around poems, later via email, and over the last three years via Zoom. He taught me much about reading and responding to poems with insight and care and has made me a better poet.

Since retiring, my husband Karl and I make regular visits to the Hudson Valley and enjoy a meal and a walk with Jay and Ingrid. Last November, we walked along the Wallkill River in New Paltz. It was chilly and dry and there was a lovely light behind the clouds in the northwest. A few days ago, Karl and I hung streams of prayer flags we had bought at a shop by that trailhead. I tied my end to a strong rope of ivy braided around an aspen thinking of Jay and how, now, those flags are uttering prayers for him.

–Jamie O'Halloran

Jamie O'Halloran is the author of *Corona Connemara & Half a Crown.*

Schoodic Point

The Atlantic sweeps from the horizon
to where basalt from a long-extinct volcano fissures
slabs of speckled granite that drop in shelves
to the great pounding waves.

They crest and shatter into cloudbursts of fine spray
that falls on the rocks
and into channels between the rocks
and settles in swirls of green.

We sit for a long time, wrapped
in the heat of sun and stone
and the percussion of the waves
as they explode and subside, explode and subside.

Summer

Year after year we come back
to the soughing and sighing of the wind
in the leaves of the oaks and pines,
to the play of shadow and light.

Night after night we walk out into the field
to breathe the scent of grass and turn our faces
up to the round eye of night,
or the sickle of the new moon
and the brilliance of our galaxy.

Year after year we return to our mountains
to climb to their granite crowns
and look down on the green hills, the dark ponds,
the seacoast, the shadows of clouds
moving over them, our sustenance.

-- Ingrid Blaufarb Hughes

Ingrid Blaufarb Hughes is the author of *Losing Aaron*, a memoir
about her son's life and schizophrenia.

Acknowledgements

Over the years, previous versions of these poems have appeared in a number of magazines and literary journals, including: *Agni, The American Literary Review, Vegetable Box, The Bellingham Review, Hanging Loose, Beloit Poetry Journal, Shark Reef, Terra Nova, The Devil's Millhopper, Heliotrope, Silkworm, Shark Reef, One Hand Clapping,* and *The Main Street Rag.*

Author Note

Jay Klokker was born and raised on the shores of Puget Sound, in Bremerton, Washington, the son of a naval architect at the Puget Sound Naval Shipyard. He received a BA from Fairhaven College of Western Washington University, and a MA in creative writing at Boston University.

For most of his adult life he taught, first college students at the University of Washington, later at Boston University, and then for thirty years at the Adult Learning Center of the New York City University College of Technology, where he was a beloved teacher of adult basic education, high school equivalency, and English to immigrants.

Jay and his wife Ingrid Blaufarb Hughes spent most of the year in New Paltz, NY, and summers in Surry, Maine, where Jay pursued his lifelong interest in hiking, bird watching and being part of the natural world.

www.ingramcontent.com/pod-product-compliance
Lightning Source LLC
Chambersburg PA
CBHW021348090426
42742CB00008B/783